EVERYTHING I WANTED TO KNOW ABOUT GOD I LEARNED FROM MY CATS

A Book About Growing Your Relationship With God through Your Relationship with Your Pets

Rev. William E. Anderson

Copyright 2024, William E. Anderson

All rights reserved. No part of this book may be reproduced or transmitted in any form or by any means, mechanical or electronic, including photocopying, or by any information storage and retrieval system without written permission from the author.

Scripture quotes used with permission based on Gratis Use or Fair Use from publishers:

NKJV: Scripture taken from the New King James Version®. Copyright ©1982 by Thomas Nelson. Used by permission. All rights reserved.

NLT: Holy Bible: New Living Translation, Copyright ©2006. Used by permission of Tyndale House Publishers. All rights reserved.

NASB: Scripture quotations taken from the (NASB®) New American Standard Bible®, Copyright © 1960, 1971, 1977, 1995, 2020 by The Lockman Foundation. Used by permission. All rights reserved. lockman.org

KJV: Scripture taken from the Authorized King James Version®. Copyright ©1769, in Public Domain.

William E. Anderson

E-mail: derputz@aol.com

18950 Consul Ave.

Corona, CA 92881

Publisher's Cataloging-in-Publication Data

Name: Anderson, William E., 1940- Author

Title: Everything I wanted to know about God I learned from my cats, A Book About Your Relationship With God/ by William E. Anderson.

Description: [Corona, California] : [William E. Anderson], [2024] : Interest age level: 010-095.

Summary: The author compares the relationship with between pets and people with a relationship with God.

Identifier: ISBN 9781736311530 (paperback) [ISBN 978173611547 (ebook)

Printed in the U.S.A.

Contents

FORWARD 5
What It's All About 6
Sancho 14
Rusty 17
Lucky 21
Pepper 24
Mittens 26
Daisy 28
Cocoa 31
Cupcake 34
Snuggles 42
Pepsi 46
Trouble 48
Burrito 50
God and Sancho 53
Lessons from Cupcake & the Cats 58
L'envoi 95

FORWARD

I love my pets. They depend on me to meet all their needs, and I depend on God to meet all my needs. I wrote this book to show others how we can love God more as we observe our feelings toward our pets. Included in the chapters are scripture references for each example I've observed in how God teaches us about his love for us, our love for him, and our love for everyone else, including the animals.

The LORD has used experiences with my pets to teach me how much He loves me and how He wants to be loved by me. I pray you and your family will grow closer to God as you read this book and examine the God's gift of animals in your life.

What It's All About

This is NOT a book about cats. It is a book about relationships. Specifically, it is about your relationship with your God and mine.

We love both our children and our pets. Our relationship with our children is often complicated. We love and discipline them. Parents help teach and mold their kids into healthy adults. We try to instill good values in our children. Our job as parents is to raise them to be adults we and society can be proud of. It ain't easy!

Thankfully, our relationships with our pets are much simpler to analyze. Dogs and cats give unconditional love. They look to us for everything: food, water, affection, and protection. It is our responsibility to meet their every need. That's when it struck me, don't we look to God to do all that for us?

God made us to love. This love extends to all his creation, including the animals. The bond between humans and animals can as very strong as between those between two people. Remember Roy Rogers and his horse, Trigger. Think about your relationship about your dog or cat. How do they make you feel? What would you do to help them or protect them? What things do you do for them each day?

God made us to love.

Now, think about how your pets love you unconditionally. When you return home, they greet you with great joy. If you are rude or mean toward them, they still continue to show you love and affection. Their desire is to please you. Similarly, your greatest desire should be to please God. Our relationship with God should be like this. You could think of it as we are God's pets and should love and follow Him the way our pets do us. And in the same way we take care of our pet's needs, so God takes care of us.

God is our owner, and we are His children.

Let us consider what God said in the scripture:

And God blessed them, and God said unto them [man], Be fruitful, and multiply, and replenish the earth, and subdue it: and have dominion over the fish of the sea, and over the fowl of the air, and over every living thing that moveth upon the earth.

Genesis 1:28 KJV

And out of the ground the LORD God formed every beast of the field, and every fowl of the air; and brought them unto Adam to see what he would call them: and whatsoever Adam called every living creature, that was the name thereof.

Genesis 2:19 KJV

These two verses explain God gave man dominion over all animals. We were made responsible to care for the garden of Eden and all life in it. The care of all animals is our responsibility. This gives us authority to decide life or death over animals, but not to harm or abuse them. We are called to give our animals good care. God provided animals to us to help bear our burdens, to be our companions, and for food. He gave us wild animals to look at with awe and respect to realize the vast variety of God's creation.

When we use animals to pull wagons, to plow, to pack, or to ride, we will get the most assistance from them when we treat them humanely. If we do not, God will take up their cause against us. Consider the story of Balak who was hired by the king of the Amorites to curse Israel.

Balaam got up in the morning, saddled his donkey and went with the Moabite officials. But God was very angry when he went, and the angel of the LORD stood in the road to oppose him. Balaam was riding on his donkey, and his two servants were with him. When the donkey saw the angel of the LORD standing in the road with a drawn sword in his hand, it turned off the road into a field. Balaam beat it to get it back on the road. Then the angel of the LORD stood in a narrow path through the vineyards, with walls on both sides. When the donkey saw the angel of the LORD, it pressed close to the wall, crushing Balaam's foot against it. So he beat the donkey again. Then the angel of the LORD moved on ahead and stood in a narrow place where there was no room to turn, either to the right or to the left. When the donkey saw the angel of the LORD, it lay down under Balaam, and he was angry and beat it with his staff.

Then the LORD opened the donkey's mouth, and it said to Balaam, "What have I done to you to make you beat me these three times?"

Balaam answered the donkey, "You have made a fool of me! If only I had a sword in my hand, I would kill you right now."

The donkey said to Balaam, "Am I not your own donkey, which you have always ridden, to this day? Have I been in the habit of doing this to you?"

"No," he said.

Then the LORD opened Balaam's eyes, and he saw the angel of the LORD standing in the road with his sword drawn. So he bowed low and fell facedown.

The angel of the LORD asked him, "Why have you beaten your donkey these three times? I have come here to oppose you because your path is a reckless one before me. The donkey saw me and turned away from me these three times. If it had not turned away, I would certainly have killed you by now, but I would have spared it."

Balaam said to the angel of the LORD, "I have sinned. I did not realize you were standing in the road to oppose me. Now if you are displeased, I will go back."

Numbers 22:21-34 NIV

In the story, Balaam's donkey was more wise than he was. The donkey tried to protect his owner, while Balaam unaware of the danger before him tried to force his will upon the donkey to move in the direction he wanted.

By the end of the story though, Balaam repents and admits his sin of abusing the donkey, showing us it is not acceptable to harm God's animals out of anger.

Animals raised for food must also be treated humanely, but animals, even our pets, are not equal to human beings. We can love our animals, but we must not elevate them above people.

Mankind is the highest form of life that God created. We bear the image of God within ourselves. Even, the most despicable homeless bum lying drunk on the street is still a man Jesus died for. God loves and cares for all His animals and all His creation. He declared all creation "good." But, after the creation of man, He called it "very good." God gives us the privilege of tending and caring for His garden and all the creatures in it, but they should never be exalted above a person.

We can't elevate animals above people.

I am a pastor, now retired, and live on one acre of land in California. I help to care for a lady, named Cyndi, who has another house on the property. She has operated a wildlife rescue facility on the land for over thirty years now. Together, we have rescued hawks, owls, egrets, ducks, songbirds, and many other birds, plus squirrels, rabbits, raccoons, skunks, and other small wild mammals. We do not rehabilitate domestic animals, only those which can be released back into the wild.

My friend, Cyndi, has a magical touch caring for animals and birds. We are now too old to keep up with taking every kind of animal in to nurture and have cut back to only taking baby Mallard ducks. We also have currently one dog named Rusty and nine cats.

This is the story of how I learned much of the nature of God from caring for our pets.

I have always been blessed with animals in my life, starting around two years of age when I had a little stuffed dog with only one eye named Blackie. I grew up with canaries and parakeets.

Before I dive into the lessons I've learned about God from my pets, I want to introduce you to my fur family of critters. It has always amazed me to see the variety of different personalities in each individual dog and cat. In California, we have many coyotes in our local area, so all our cats live indoors, always. Some of the cats take more to Cyndi, others to me. Rusty clings to both of us. Most of our fur family are females, with only two males in the house.

Sancho

Sancho was a very special dog. She died several years ago. It was through Sancho that I first realized the parallel between my relationship with her and my relationship with God. She was a black, female Basenji with a curly tail and a purple tongue indicating some Chow descendancy in her bloodline. Sancho owned our truck. She climbed all over it and sat on Cyndi's lap everywhere we went. Every time we went to *In & Out Burgers*, one of our favorite restaurants, Cyndi had to be very careful. If Cyndi turned her head to look at something, Sancho would grab a hunk of her hamburger. It was impossible to get mad at Sancho though. She sat on Cyndi's lap with a big grin, licking her chops. Once Sancho grabbed a steak off the table. She was always so proud of herself.

When she was still a puppy, she chewed up three of my tennis shoes. She also liked to chew the wooden legs of our kitchen table. We tried painting the legs with Bitter Apple liquid from the pet store. She liked it! Someone suggested cayenne pepper hot sauce. She liked that better. Finally, she outgrew the chewing urge but the table legs are still all chewed up.

Sancho

One time as we were waiting at a stoplight, five young punks started to surround the truck. One came up on the left; one went behind; another crossed to the right side, and two others stood right in front of the truck. I put the truck in gear and prepared to run the red light out of fear we were about to be carjacked. But before I could move, Sancho suddenly jumped up from Cyndi's lap. She bared her teeth, barking and growling at the men. She knew they were up to no good and did not like them at all. Boy, you never saw five guys disappear faster in your life!

We always had to walk Sancho with a leash. If not, she would disappear over the hill and be very hard to get back. One time, as we walked her on the trail, she saw something ahead that scared her and started barking. The only thing ahead of us was an old shot up metal sign. When we got closer, Sancho saw that it was just a sign. She couldn't admit that she was barking at a silly sign so she walked past the sign barking at some fictitious thing further down the path. She wouldn't admit that was wrong about the sign.

Sancho was always especially close to me and followed me everywhere. She spent most nights sleeping on my bed near my feet.

Even though it has been several years since her death, I still miss her.

Rusty

Rusty is a Vizsla with a touch of Beagle in her. She is our current dog. Vizslas are very energetic and rambunctious Hungarian hunting dogs with floppy ears. When we first got her from the shelter, we didn't know what breed she was. A friend suggested she might be a Vizsla. Googling "Vizsla" online produced several videos of Vizslas.

The first two videos showed a medium-sized, brown dog running over sofas, jumping over chairs, and sliding across the living room floor. Rusty did all that. She would zip around the house all over the furniture and slide into the back door when she stopped. The videos fit Rust's personality and appearance.

Another video showed another "Rusty"

swimming in a swimming pool. That dog would dive to the bottom of the pool. Then it ran out of the pool, ran around the yard, and jumped back in with a mighty dive.

Our neighbor has a beautiful swimming pool, and they let us use it anytime. They loved watching Rusty swim in the pool. Like the video dogs, Rusty loves to swim.

Rusty

We would also bring our two geese, Adam and Eve, to the pool with Rusty. The geese swam around serenely for a while, then Rusty would make a great running leap into the water after them. The geese would dive under water while Rusty dog-paddled around looking for them.

Where did they go? She wondered.

Then the geese would pop up on the other side of the pool. Rusty would swim toward them, and before she got too close, the geese would disappear again. The ducks repeated their game of hide-and-seek over and over again until Rusty would get finally tired and leave the pool to rest. She never ever got close to the geese. It was good exercise for both Rusty and the geese. It seemed they had a lot of fun.

Rusty was definitely a Vizsla.

She also is a great help around the house. Our rescue cat, Snuggles, likes to slip out of the door whenever she can. When she does, we just call, "Rusty!"

Rusty comes running and chases Snuggles out of the yard, pushing her into the house through the door with her nose. Snuggles will try to hide between the legs of a stool and bat her paws at Rusty, yowling back at the top of her voice.

Rusty isn't deterred. She would grab Snuggles' leg or tail, growling and barking furiously. This evade and retrieve tactic will go on for several minutes with a terrible racket.

Rusty is Snuggles' best friend, and they rough house like this often; afterwards, they will lie down on the couch and sleep next to each other. I think Snuggles sneaks out of the house just to play with Rusty.

Rusty also helps manage the ducks. We have double doors on most of our cages and try to be very careful, but sometimes a duck will slip out. If Rusty is nearby, she will chase the duck down and bring it back into the cage in the same way she does for Snuggles. She never hurts either the ducks or the cats. The retrieving instinct is strong in Vizslas.

Lucky

Our neighbor, Chuck, had an obviously pregnant cat who showed up while he was working in his garage. He fed her, and she kept coming back day after day. One very hot day, Cyndi was talking with Chuck and the cat showed up, very unpregnant.

Knowing the cat must have recently had her kittens, Cyndi went on the hunt.

Where were the kittens? She wondered.

She finally found them under a tarpaulin on a neighbor's porch. They were very overheated. She knocked on the door and asked the owner about the cat.

"I didn't know I even had a cat, let alone kittens," he said.

Cyndi showed him the cats on his back porch.

The next thing I knew, Cyndi showed up at my house with her arms full of kittens. "Look what I found," she announced.

Lucky, the mother cat, and her four kittens moved in with us. Cyndi eventually found a home for one of the kittens. We ended up with Lucky and her children: Pepper, the boy, and Mittens and Daisy, the girls.

Lucky died a few years ago, but her kids still live with us.

Lucky

Lucky's Kittens from left to right: Mittens, Daisy, Pepper

Pepper

Pepper is one of our two male cats. Their names are Pepper, the older cat, and Pepsi. I don't know why in the world we named them that way. They both get called "Pep" as a nickname, and we are always getting their names mixed up.

Pepper is a gentle giant. Both he and Pepsi are big boys, but Pepper is usually easy-going and gets along with the other cats. Several cats like to sleep in the large cat beds on our counter. We often laugh at Pepper sleeping with Pepsi or big 'ole Mittens.

They are all three large cats and typically sleep really scrunched together. Pepper can often be found playing with his favorite cat toy, a stuffed possum, and whining at the top of his voice.

Pepper

All of our animals are spayed or neutered but Pepper and Cupcake are very close to each other and often sleep together. They are a pair of lovers but sometimes one gets mad at the other. Cupcake always wins. She is the alpha cat.

Pepper and Cupcake

Mittens

Mittens grew into a very large and lazy piggy who mostly lays about and eats. Initially, she was as active as her brother and sister, but as she got older and fatter, she got lazy. Mittens is a bi-color cat who has a dark gray back with a white underbelly and a gray and white face. She is gentle and easy going and loves being petted. It takes two of us to lift her up to put her into the wheeled cat carrier when she has to go the vet.

She is usually found laying in her bed. Mittens eats a lot more than the other cats and moves a lot less. Sometimes, we have to put the food next to her bed to eat. When she does decide to move around the room, she will jump from the counter onto the table. When she lands, all the stuff on the table leaps about a half-foot into the

Mittens

air. Her small body can shake the place like an earthquake.

Mittens lies by the corner of kitchen counter, and when I walk by, she rolls her head way back, looks at me, and gives a little meow, asking me to pet her. She then bends her head back so that I can rub and scratch under her chin. Cats love that, to be scratched under the chin. Mittens is very affectionate.

Sadly, her health is not good. She has kidney problems and visits the vet quite often. Thankfully, she is not in pain and holding her own.

Daisy

Daisy is small, light and shy. She is marked like Pepper with a white ring around her tail. She usually stays somewhere out of sight. She loves for me to lift her up onto the top shelf of my closet. Mittens spends many hours hiding in the closet with her best buddy, Trouble. Both are about the same size and weight.

Daisy is a timid cat. She is thin and very light. I often confuse her with Pepper. Even though she is much smaller, her markings are similar. Sometimes the best way to identify her is by the little white ring halfway up her tail.

She stays in my bedroom a lot but seldom comes to me to be petted. She will tell me that she wants me to lift her up to the top shelf of my closet, then run away most times when I go to pick her up. Then, if I have my shirt on, Trouble will jump onto the desk, onto my back then into the closet shelf with Daisy. Trouble is too ADHD to stay with her very long but Daisy will stay up there all day, just leaving for supper.

When I feed the cats, I have to sit on the living room chair until they are finished eating. If I get up and walk toward them, Daisy will run away and hide. Later she will come back again to eat, but she still keeps her eyes on me. She is a very nice cat and her buddy-to-buddy relationship with Trouble is lovely to see.

Daisy

She has one little cat toy that she loves more than anything. She will carry it in her mouth, whining loudly, very proud of herself. But she drops the toy and hides if I come walking by.

Cocoa

One day we had to pick up a Red Tail hawk from the animal shelter. Cyndi went into the shelter while I waited in the truck. When Cyndi came back, she had two carriers. One had the hawk and the other had a nearly black cat.

Cyndi had run into a lady who was giving the cat to the shelter. The shelter receptionist guaranteed that it was a "No-kill shelter" but Cyndi wasn't taking any chances. So we adopted Cocoa, a young, Russian Blue cat, adding her to our growing animal family.

Cocoa usually spends the day at my house with the other cats, but Cyndi carries Cocoa to her house when she goes the bed each night. Cocoa is very vocal, meowing loudly each time either of us pass by her. She loves being petted but just up to

Cocoa

a certain point. Then she hisses or bats at you with her paw.

Our helper was petting her one day until Cocoa had enough. Cocoa batted her in the face so hard that her glasses flew across to the other side of the room! The poor girl wouldn't go near Cocoa for two weeks.

Cocoa is one of the three cats at our house that will drink out of a dripping faucet. Cupcake and Trouble are the other two cats who drink from the faucet.

When Cocoa is thirsty, she will go sit beside the sink and whine until we come and turn it on for her to get a fresh drink of water.

Cyndi is always leaving the faucets on a low drip in the kitchen and bathroom for the cats. My main job around the house is to follow Cyndi around and turn off the faucets and lights.

Cupcake

Cupcake was my special calico cat. She was very pretty, with a beautiful mix of patches of black, brown, and white and long white whiskers. Other cats can be pushy when they want attention or food, but not Cupcake. She would sit on the sink and wait for me to come by to trickle the water for her.

Some of our cats have special diets so we feed them all at the same time in order to referee the cats to make sure everyone eats what they are supposed to eat. All except Cupcake. She would jump on the table for us to feed her any time she was hungry. She marched to the beat of a different drummer.

Cupcake was so spoiled that we gave her dinner in bed often. Much of the fun of having her was spoiling her, and she enjoyed it very much. So did I.

Cupcake was the alpha cat of the house. Even our dog, Rusty, deferred to her. While Cupcake loved to eat, it was sometimes hard to get Rusty to eat her dinner. If she just sat and looked at her bowl too long, we would put Cupcake by the bowl. Out of jealously, Rusty would start to eat. After a while, we learned all we had to do was call for Cupcake to get Rusty to eat.

Cuppy loved to play. She would crawl into an empty grocery bag on the floor. Then I would pick up the bag and swing her around and around for several minutes. When I stopped, I would peek into the bag, and she would be laying there on her back staring up at me.

"Do it again, Daddy." she seemed to say.

So, I would swing her around until my arms were tired. Cupcake thought it was great fun! She also liked to lay on my swivel desk chair. I would spin it around for a minute or so. When I stopped, Cuppy just laid there ready to go again.

Any other cat would have run away from such treatment. There aren't too many cats that like to spin. I would do it over and over again, but I don't think she even got dizzy. Cupcake never seemed to suffer any ill effects from spinning.

Cupcake

Often, I would come into a room to find Cupcake sitting on the floor waiting for me. That is how she would Shanghai me. Her special look always just melted my heart. I would say, "Let's go play, 'Lassie', Cupcake," and she would lead me to whatever she wanted. Often that would be to my bed, where she wanted me to lie down with her. Cuppy loved companionship.

Cupcake would sleep with me in my bed but usually far enough away that I could barely reach her tail. Then we would play "Tailsy," as she flicked her tail back and forth like a game as I tried to pet it.

She even took over the laundry. When I brought warm laundry in from the dryer and set it upon the bed, Cupcake would jump in and curl up in the warm clothes. Sometimes she stayed there for two or three days, seldom leaving a basket of new laundry. I couldn't bring myself to chase her out of it because she looked so comfortable. Instead, I had to snake the clothes from under her when I got dressed. I usually wore wrinkly clothes decorated with cat hair.

Some of my best memories are of Cupcake with her head tilted sideways, framed by the faucet with her little pink tongue flicking out to lick the trickle of water running down. She liked my attention so I would always stand there and watch her drinking. She drank a lot and often. I think that she just wanted to keep me by the sink.

Cupcake drinking

Cupcake also liked to lay under my desk a lot. When I got ready for bed, I would call her and she would run into the bedroom and jump onto the bed to wait for me. Many times she would not come, no matter how much I begged her. Cats can be very stubborn. Nobody can herd a group of cats.

She even wanted to eat the food I ate. When we were making a sandwich in the kitchen, she would steal the ham and run. She even ate the lettuce.

Cupcake with Cyndi

Nothing ever seemed to bother Cupcake. Turn on the vacuum, and she never even flinched. Drop something, and she would just turn her head to look at you. Cyndi could do anything to her when caring for her. Cutting toenails with cats is usually a struggle. Cupcake would complain at being restrained, whining loudly, but she would hold still until her nails were done. Cupcake's ears seemed to get dirty a lot, and Cyndi would clean them with Q-tips. Cupcake laid still in her arms and purred as Cyndi cleaned her!

I usually slept with the main door open with the screen door closed to let the fresh air in during the summer. One night I was awakened by the screeching of a cat fight. I got up and found all the cats lined up looking out the screen door. They were very upset. I counted cats and found Cupcake missing. She was nowhere in the house.

Coyotes and even bobcats frequent our area. We had lost some ducks and chickens to them in the past. Something must have pushed the door open from the outside allowing Cupcake to get out. Cyndi and I searched all over the yard for over an hour without any luck. I even went up the hill with a flashlight expecting to find her body lying dead on the trail from the predators. My heart was broken. I had lost my Cupcake.

We were just ready to give up and go home when Cyndi heard something faint in the distance. We both listened to see where the sound came from. It was a feeble meow. We found Cupcake on a table under a tree in front of my house. Relieved beyond belief, I carried her back into my house. The skin on her back was ripped open and there were bite marks on her neck. We went to the veterinarian the next day to get her patched up. Thankfully, she recovered fully, and I had my precious Cupcake back. It still makes me shudder when I think of that night.

We later learned that one neighbor had a very mean cat which was free to roam the neighborhood. We figured this cat must have come to our door and pushed it open. Cuppy, being the lead cat, would have confronted the intruder first and must have been dragged out the door in a fight. The next day I fixed the door so that it could not be pushed open from the outside. I thank God that Cupcake was saved.

Because we were so close, Cupcake is the cat who taught me the most about my relationship with God. She is absolutely my best friend.

Cupcake on a bag

Snuggles

Snuggles is a long-haired Calico cat. She is small, light and very active. I met her in the shelter where I was helping the staff to euthanize an injured Red-tail hawk. I had to keep the hawk from biting or grabbing Bridget, the shelter officer, while she injected the bird. While we waited for the bird to pass, I leaned back against a cage and felt a cat paw grabbing at my arm. It was Snuggles. I petted her and she rubbed against my arm.

A couple of days later, when I was in the shelter again, I told Bridget I would take that Calico if no one else had spoken for her.

Bridget said, "I am glad you said something. We were going to put her down in about ten minutes, after you leave. Oh, by the way, she is pregnant."

A few days later Snuggles gave birth to five kittens. Three died early, and we kept the other two. We named the black and white tuxedo, Pepsi, and the other kitten, another Calico like its mother except with short hair, we called Trouble.

Snuggles really loves people. She jumps on everyone's lap or shoulder and tries to sneak out the door on their head. She is the only one of our cats that sneaks out the door if we are not careful. If she manages sneak out, Rusty will run after her and herd Snuggles back into the house with her nose. Then Rusty will chase her around the house.

Snuggles

Snuggles will seek refuge between the rungs of a chair or stool, screeching and batting back at Rusty while Rusty grabs a leg or tail. Rusty growls and barks loudly. From a distance, the whole affair looks like a full-on cat and dog fight, but that's not really true.

Actually, Rusty and Snuggles are the best of friends and this loud and boisterous tussle is how they play. We think this is the real reason Snuggles sneaks outside. She loves to play with Rusty. If Snuggles gets bored and Rusty doesn't want to play, Snuggles will chase her tail around and around on the chair.

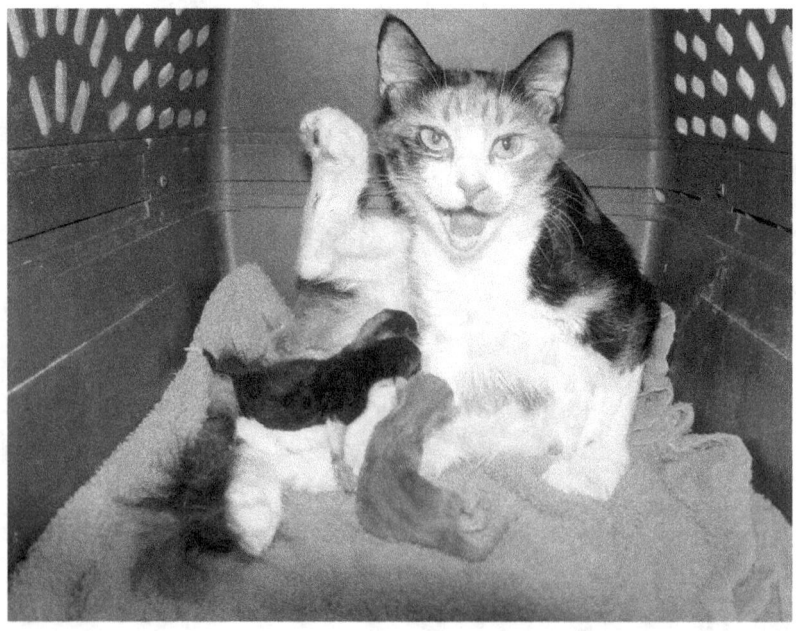

Snuggles with her kittens

Every day, when I wake up, I find Snuggy laying on my tummy. It must be the softest place in the house. If I lie down during the day, she will hop on my tummy just about the time I want to get up. I don't know how she always picks this timing, but, as every cat owner knows, you just cannot kick a cat off of your lap. This gives me a good excuse to lay there longer.

Pepsi

Pepsi is a large male, tuxedo cat, much larger than his mother. He has ADHD and is very active. Sometimes he can be pushy but he is very loving and cuddly.

Lately, he has been sleeping next to me most nights. When he first started to sleep with me, he couldn't settle down. First, he would lay on my right side. A few minutes later, he would get up to lay on my left side between my arm and my side. Then he would begin to kneed my arm until it started to hurt.

When I would stop him, and he would move back to my right side for a while. Then we would start the cycle all over again. Finally, I put my hand on his back and get him to settle down. Nowadays, he just lies on the right of me and goes to sleep quickly. He doesn't like me to pet him on his head, just his back.

Pepsi is more comfortable with Cyndi than me. He loves to sit on her lap when she watches television.

Pepsi

Trouble

Trouble and Daisey both love to spend the majority of their days on the top shelf of my closet. Daisey will sit in front of the closet and meow for me to pick her up to lift her up onto the top shelf. I am glad she is so light. After that, Trouble wants up on the shelf too. She jumps up to the desk right beside the closet and mews at me. I bend over and lean next to the desk beside her. After some hesitation, I coax her to hop onto my back. Then I straighten up and she hops up onto the shelf.

The other cats occasionally have little squabbles with each other, but never Trouble. She is very active, with maybe a touch of her brother's ADHD, but she never gets into any trouble.

Her name is ironic because with a name like Trouble, you'd expect her to be in trouble a lot. But, Trouble never lived up to her namesake, being one of the kindest and non-aggressive cats.

As I write this, Trouble is just about bald. The hair on her back tends to get tangled and cannot be brushed out. We took her to the vet, and they shaved off all her hair, except for the tip of her tail. She sure looks funny missing all her hair. I wonder if she must have been all hair, because she is so skinny now!

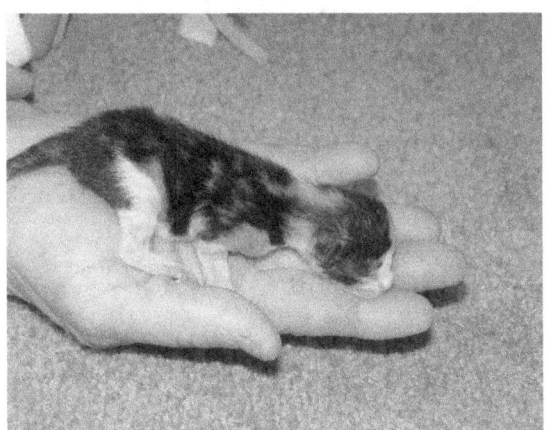

Baby Trouble

Trouble as an adult

Burrito

Burrito is our youngest cat. She was found by a friend one rainy day lying in the gutter outside her house. Burrito had just been born and was freezing cold and barely alive. Our friend had to go out of town for the weekend and asked Cyndi to take care of her until she returned.

"I promise that I will take the cat back when I return. I won't stick you with another cat."

We nursed Burrito back to good health for over three weeks. When Cyndi's friend returned, in spite of her promise, we decided to keep Burrito.

Burrito was so sick and bloated that we had her in the veterinarian's office every day for a week. The vet brought her to us and shook his head. He didn't think the kitten would make live either, but slowly she got better.

One day we had her with us over at a friend's house. Cyndi went out to get Burrito some milk. She came back with Burrito all wrapped in a towel with her head sticking out the end. We all looked at her and shouted in unison, "It's a burrito."

And that is how Burrito got her name.

Later, the friend who had found little Burrito got Cyndi a tee shirt with a picture of a cat wrapped up in a tortilla which read, "They told me I could be anything I wanted and I want to be a burrito."

It was perfect.

Burrito is the fluffiest cat I have ever seen. She is mostly a white Himalayan cat with a few small brown spots and a very fluffy tail. She leaves hair floating in the air everywhere she goes.

She has a favorite place to be fed—on a little

Burrito

end table in the living room. Strangely, she never goes into the kitchen or on the counter where the other cats hang out.

Unfortunately, since Burrito is the last cat to enter the pack, she is at the bottom of the pecking order. The other cats sometimes pick on her. She usually stays by herself and is very quiet. Burrito stays primarily in the living room and bedroom. She used to climb into bed with me at night and crawl under the covers. Lately however, she has begun to pee and poop on the bed and the couch so that we have had to put a plywood cover on them to keep her off. We still love her and pet her, but have not been able to change this behavior.

God and Sancho

I first realized the parallel of our relationship to our pets and God's relationship with us when my dog, Sancho, had a tumor removed from her side. The biopsy showed it was cancerous. The veterinarian sadly had not gotten all of it.

Sancho did very well with the first operation, but she was in terrible pain after the second one. She could not sit still. She moved from room to room and chair to couch trying to get comfortable. I followed her around, petting her and trying to calm her down and give her comfort.

She finally settled down under my desk, and I pulled up a sleeping bag next to her to spend the night with her. As I petted Sancho, I said to her, "I know you don't understand why I did this to you. I love you. You cannot understand why you are hurting like this, but you know me and trust me. I would never hurt you unless it was really necessary."

My heart was aching for Sancho, and I wanted desperately to help her. About this time, while I was under my desk, I felt a hand rest on my shoulder and a voice said, "My son, that is what I have been trying to tell you for years."

It was a little shocking.

Then it finally sank in. I should look to God the same way Sancho looks to me. And I understood how God feels when I am hurting or disobedient.

After this experience, I started to notice things my dogs or cats did that taught me something about God and how to understand my relationship with Him better.

I heard a Christian radio commentator today talking about the way people call themselves "Mommy" or "Daddy" to their pets. He said, "You are not your dog's parent. You own your dog."

We call God, "Abba, Father." He owns us if we choose to follow and obey Him. We are like gods to our pets, and they look to us as fathers and mothers.

After years of riding in our truck and hiking

Sancho

in the mountains in summer and snow, Sancho got old. Arthritis slowed her down, and she hung around with me even more.

She was old and hurting badly. It was finally time to do what was necessary to ease her pain. It was so hard to walk into the vet's office, but it was inconceivable to let Sancho die alone. I also knew I couldn't let her suffering continue. She was my responsibility. After she was gone, I sat crying for half an hour.

I work with a lady who rehabilitates all kinds of wild animals. Many animals and birds come to us with broken wings, broken legs, and even broken backs. When their injuries are too severe to be helped, they must be euthanized. I hate it. It is always a hard decision to make.

God has given us the authority over animals, to care for them, even over their life and death. It is a terrible responsibility. God has this kind of responsibility over us. I cannot begin to imagine having to decide when a person should die. God makes these decisions every day, and His timing is perfect. He is never wrong.

I wish I could be so confident when I make such decisions, but unlike God, I am not omnipotent or infallible.

Lesson 1
Authority equals responsibility.

And out of the ground the LORD God formed every beast of the field, and every fowl of the air; and brought them unto Adam to see what he would call them: and whatsoever Adam called every living creature, that was the name thereof.

Genesis 2:19 KJV

Adam's naming of the animals represents mankind's authority over them. With our authority comes a great responsibility to lovingly care for all animals.

Lessons from Cupcake & the Cats

**Lesson 2
Ask and I will receive.**

Cupcake is never hesitant to ask me for anything. She shows me what she wants and if I am busy, she just sits there and waits for me.

Ye have not, because ye ask not.
James 4:2 KJV

Lesson 3
Wait on the Lord.

The waiting part is the hardest part of life.

Wait on the LORD: be of good courage, and he shall strengthen thine heart: wait, I say, on the LORD.
Psalm 27:14 KJV

Lesson 4
Sit at the Lord's feet.

Cupcake is a "Mary" type of personality. She loves to simply lie by my feet and just be in my presence.

Now it came to pass, as they went, that he entered into a certain village: and a certain woman named Martha received him into her house. And she had a sister called Mary, which also sat at Jesus' feet, and heard his word. But Martha was cumbered about much serving, and came to him, and said, Lord, dost thou not care that my sister hath left me to serve alone? Bid her therefore that she help me.

And Jesus answered and said unto her, Martha, Martha, thou art careful and troubled about many things But one thing is needful: and Mary hath chosen that good part, which shall not be taken away from her.

Luke 10:37-42 KJV

Lesson 5
Be delighted daily in the Lord.

Just as I am about to get up and do something, Cupcake rolls on her back to ask for a tummy rub. She lies there and purrs as I scratch her belly, and I, of course, delight in pleasing her.

Then I was by him, [as] one brought up [with him]: and I was daily [his] delight, rejoicing always before him.

Proverbs 8:30 KJV

Lesson 6
Rest in the Lord's love for me.

Cupcake doesn't do anything useful—she doesn't catch mice or kill spiders. She just lies around looking cute, especially when she is asleep. But when I look at her my heart just melts. I don't do much for the Lord either but I know that sometimes He just looks down at me and smiles. Sometimes He laughs.

The LORD thy God in the midst of thee is mighty; he will save, he will rejoice over thee with joy; he will rest in his love, he will joy over thee with singing.
Zephaniah 3:17 KJV

**Lesson 7
God loves to provide for me.**

It gives me great pleasure to make Cupcake purr, by petting her or just laying down beside her. I believe it pleases my Father when He makes me purr.

Delight thyself also in the LORD; and he shall give thee the desires of thine heart.

Psalms 37:4 KJV

Lesson 8
Put my trust in God.

Cupcake has enormous trust in Cyndi and me. Today Cupcake was sleeping in a box in the closet when Cyndi started to vacuum a couple of feet from her. Any of the other cats would have run out in a flash but not Cupcake— she just lay there purring. I wish that I trusted my Father that much.

Blessed [are] all they that put their trust in him.
Psalm 2:12 KJV

Lesson 9
Keep God's commandments.

I asked Cupcake, "Do you love me?" She softly purrs in contentment. Then I answered myself, "I know you love me by the look in your eyes and the way you act.

If ye love me, keep my commandments.
John 14:15 KJV

Lesson 10
God has infinite love for me.

I love Cupcake so much that I cannot get mad at her. I could never get angry at Sancho either, even when she grabbed a hamburger from my hand. I love these guys so much. But God's love for me is infinitely more than my love for them.

For I am persuaded, that neither death, nor life, nor angels, nor principalities, nor powers, nor things present, nor things to come, Nor height, nor depth, nor any other creature, shall be able to separate us from the love of God, which is in Christ Jesus our Lord.

Romans 8:38-39 KJV

Lesson 11
The Lord is merciful to me.

Some times when I come into a room, Cupcake will lift her head and just look at me. I get a warm, loving feeling and it reminds me to look at God that way.

So our eyes [look] to the LORD our God, Until He has mercy on us.

Psalms 123:2 NKJV

Lesson 12
I depend on the Lord.

Cupcake thinks she is very independent. She can totally ignore me when I call her. But she totally depends on me. People like to think that they are independent too, but they are not. They depend on God, whether they know it or not.

So now, come back to your God. Act with love and justice, and always depend on him.

Hosea 12:6 NLT

Lesson 13
The Lord delights in me.

"I love you so much." I say this often to Cupcake as I pet her. She looks so lovable, especially when she is sleeping with her head upside down or with her paws covering her eyes against the light.

This is how the Father loves us. He calls us the apple of His eye. He delights in us just like I delight in Cupcake. Cupcake is very special … and so am I.

For the LORD delights in you.
                              Isaiah 62:4 NASB

Lesson 14
God loves me with an everlasting love.

I told her, "I'll always love you. I hope you will be good and stay out of trouble. But good or bad, I'll always love you, just because you are my Cupcake. This is the same thing God says to me.

The LORD hath appeared of old unto me, [saying], Yea, I have loved thee with an everlasting love: therefore with lovingkindness have I drawn thee.

Jeremiah 31:3 KJV

Lesson 15
The Lord delights in me.

I was in my car with the engine running when I saw Cupcake in the kitchen window wanting a drink from the faucet. I turned off the engine, went inside to turn the faucet on and waited until she was done. Isn't it wonderful that God loves us so much that He always drops whatever He is doing to meet our needs?

If ye shall ask any thing in my name, I will do [it].
John 14:14 KJV

Lesson 16
I am a child of God.

Cupcake doesn't do much; she mostly lays around and sleeps. But she never looks cuter than when she sleeps lying on her back with her feet up in the air. I look at her and my heart just melts. I love her so.

Look at Abraham's life. He just lived day-by-day, loved Sarah, and raised his sons. We don't read of him ever preaching about God and similarly of all the patriarchs. Their main accomplishments were raising their families, and their genealogical line would lead to the Messiah.

But "Abraham believed God and it was counted to him as righteousness." Just as I love Cupcake unconditionally, so I can rest in God's unconditional love.

Behold, what manner of love the Father hath bestowed upon us, that we should be called the sons of God.

1 John 3:1 KJV

Lesson 17
I am a child of God.

Today started abruptly with the early arrival of two guys delivering a new stove. Cupcake just lay on the floor under my desk throughout all the confusion. Nothing ever phases her. When I laid down on my bed after they left, I think she did feel a little uneasy because she followed me up on to the bed and lay next to me. How often when the noise and confusion of life makes us feel uncomfortable do we need to lie down and rest next to our Father in Heaven.

I am reminded of a time when J. F. Kennedy was president. He was in a staff meeting when little John-John wandered into the room. All the affairs of state came to a stop while John-John climbed up on his father's lap. We also have that great privilege to climb up on our Father's lap and find comfort at any time. He is never too busy to comfort us.

Blessed be God, even the Father of our Lord Jesus Christ, the Father of mercies, and the God of all comfort.
2 Corinthians 1:3 KJV

Lesson 18
God meets all my daily needs.

Often, I come across Cupcake looking up at me. I ask what she wants and we play "Lassie" as she leads me to the sink or table. She looks up at me with those big, black eyes asking for food or a drink. It feels so good for me to see her looking to me for all her needs and desires. I hasten to meet them.

Every day I look up to God for all my needs and desires. He hastens to grant me everything good. He delights in me and in meeting my needs and desires.

Give us this day our daily bread.
                    Matthew 6:11 KJV

Lesson 19
I belong to God.

Cupcake is getting old and clumsy. As I am going out, I always remind her, "Be careful. You are very clumsy. Remember, you belong to me. You are my most valuable object." God tells me that I belong to Him. Jesus paid a terrible price for me. I think He got ripped off, but He calls me the "pearl of great price." I am the one He sought to find. He delights in me. I am royalty and a priest to Him. I had best take care of this body which is His holy temple.

Know ye not that ye are the temple of God, and that the Spirit of God dwelleth in you?

1 Corinthians 3:16 KJV

Lesson 20
I belong to God.

Cupcake has always been an independent thinker. When she was younger, she knew what she wanted and when she wanted it. She insisted on a drink whenever she wanted it and she wanted to drink from the sink. She ate when she wanted to eat, not when we fed the other cats. Sometimes she slept on my bed with me (which I loved), but other times I could not coax her from under the desk or from one of the cat beds when it was bedtime.

As she grows older and closer to me, the things she wants became more and more the things I liked to do for her. I don't have to coax her to come to bed with me as much as I used to. She just goes in and waits for me. Likewise, I have found that as I have gotten closer to the Lord, I find what I want is what Jesus wants for me. My prayers have been less and less about me. Now I ask Him for what He wants for me. My prayers are more aligned with His will.

This is the confidence which we have before Him, that, if we ask anything according to His will, He hears us.

1 John 5:14 NASB

Lesson 21
I abide in God's love.

Cupcake is lazy. Many nights I have to carry her to bed with me. However, sometimes she surprises me by running in and hopping onto my bed. Then I am just elated! I don't want any pet that is trained to always obey me from fear. I want an animal who loves me, knows my ways and chooses to follow me.

God didn't make us to be robots. He made us to follow Him, to learn His ways, and to delight Him by being willingly obedient to Him.

If ye keep my commandments, ye shall abide in my love; even as I have kept my Father's commandments, and abide in his love.

John 15:10 KJV

Lesson 22
I allow God's will to be done in my life.

Cupcake usually sleeps in my bed with me. I enjoy that a lot. But sometimes she sleeps under my desk. I call to her, "Come on Cupcake. Let's go to bed."

But sometimes, even if I coax her, she won't come. She wants what she wants.

As I sit there coaxing her, I realize that is just like God coaxing me to do what He wants me to do. And sometimes I am just as stubborn as Cupcake and don't listen, but when I do God always blesses me.

Not my will, but thine, be done.
Luke 22:42 KJV

Lesson 23
I make the Lord happy.

Today I lost my laundry basket to Cupcake. After I do my laundry, I have to get my PJ's out quickly before Trouble or Cupcake hops into the warm clothes and parks there for the night. Yesterday, Cupcake jumped into my laundry basket and made a nest out of my clothes. She spent all night and all day there today. Eventually, I gave up trying to get the cats out of my laundry basket and finally got Cupcake her own clothes basket. She loves it!

The basket sits on my bed with me and Cupcake is super loving. She appreciates her gift a whole lot, and I am having a ball petting her and getting love-licks back. Our relationship gives joy to both of us.

My prayer tonight was, "Lord, I pray that I can make You as happy as Cupcake makes me."

The LORD thy God in the midst of thee is mighty; he will save, he will rejoice over thee with joy; he will rest in his love, he will joy over thee with singing.
                    Zephaniah 3:17 KJV

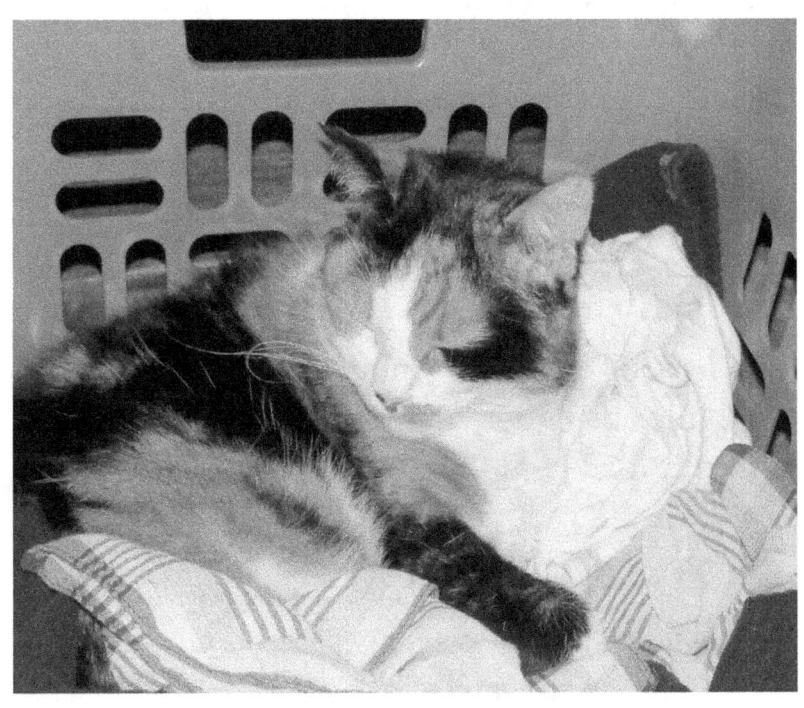

Cupcake in a laundry basket

Lesson 24
I grow more in love with God each day.

As Cupcake and I grow older together, we have grown much closer to each other. She lays beside me more often now, licks my hand more, and actually obeys me when I call her.

Likewise, as I grow older, I am eighty-two-years-old as I write this today, I have grown closer to God. I am blown away by His grace and beauty. I try to comprehend the mind that created the colors of the earth around me. I wake each morning to see the brown bark and green leaves of the tree outside my window dancing in the sunlight against a background of blue sky. I am amazed!

At this age the colors seem vibrantly alive. I feel like a child first discovering new colors for the first time in the toys his father gives him.

I see all this beauty and wonder at the world my Father has given me, and I just want to hold Him and love Him the way I do Cupcake.

And thou shalt love the Lord thy God with all thy heart, and with all thy soul, and with all thy mind, and with all thy strength: this [is] the first commandment.

Mark 12:30 KJV

Lesson 25
Sometimes I'm too stiff-necked.

My pets know who owns them. They know who feeds them and provides the world they live in. They love me but just try to order a cat to "Come!" They are stiff-necked and rebellious. They only obey when they feel like it. Much of the time they are indifferent to me, unless they want something.

The Bible calls us a "stiff-necked and rebellious people." We are often indifferent to the love overtures of God toward us.

See to it, brothers and sisters, that none of you has a sinful, unbelieving heart that turns away from the living God.

Hebrews 3:12 NIV

Lesson 26
I am not afraid when I'm with God.

My dog Sancho is long dead. Now I have another dog named Rusty. Rusty is very afraid of fireworks and loud noises. I have tried everything I know to calm her whenever there's a loud noise but to no avail. At night she follows me from room to room lying beside my feet.

Sometimes when I fear something, I cannot shake that feeling. But that is when I need to sit at the feet of my Savior. He will protect me.

When thou liest down, thou shalt not be afraid: yea, thou shalt lie down, and thy sleep shall be sweet.

Proverbs 3:24 KJV

Lesson 27
God always provides for me.

While Cupcake is the cat closest to me, I have another cat named Daisy. As I was sitting in my bedroom one day, Daisy came in and put her paws in front of her, then gave a good stretch. Watching her, I realized that she has a good life. It was a blessing to her that Daisy could relax like that. I give her food and water. Cyndi or I clean the kitty box. We give her shelter and the run of the house. We protect her and take her to the vet. Daisy, of course, takes all this for granted.

Daisy's only job is to please me.

I am sheltered, fed and watered every day. I have the freedom to go where I want and do whatever I wish to do. And for all these blessings and more, my only job is to please the Lord.

Therefore take no thought, saying, 'What shall we eat?' or, 'What shall we drink?' or, 'Wherewithal shall we be clothed?' (For after all these things do the Gentiles seek:) for your heavenly Father knoweth that ye have need of all these things.

Matthew 6:31-32 KJV

Lesson 28
I will put my trust the Lord.

Daisy, my very timid cat, comes to me daily for me to lift her up to the top shelf in the closet. Usually, when I come near her, she runs away. Today, as I lifted her up onto the closet shelf I remarked to her, "You come to me every day to lift you up, yet you usually run away from me."

The LORD told me, "That's what you do to Me."

I run away from God most of the time, but when I need or want something I go to Him and He always lifts me up.

O LORD my God, in You I put my trust; Save me from all those who persecute me.

Psalms 7:1 NASB

Lesson 29
I will trust God is good.

Daisy is so timid that when I come near, she runs away from me, even when I am feeding her. I have never hurt her in any way, yet she does not trust me. I feed her every day and I lift her up onto the top shelf of my closet, her favorite place. I only do good things for her.

Likewise, God has only done good things for me. Yet, when I screw up, I am too timid to 'fess up to Him.' I tend to run away from God when I should run toward Him. Don't I trust in God's goodness? Yes, I do. I am just like a cat.

For God hath not given us the spirit of fear; but of power, and of love, and of a sound mind.

2 Timothy 1:7 KJV

Lesson 30
God forgives my transgressions.

Burrito has turned into a brat. She pees and poops on the bed, furniture, and the floor– every night. I was beginning to think about giving Burrito away. Then the Lord reminded me the other day that I am a brat sometimes too, but He still loves me and treats me with patience and goodness. Therefore, I must continue to keep and love Burrito. I must put up with her transgressions, just like God puts up with mine.

"Lord, you made man to be Your companion, for Your pleasure. You made dogs and cats to be man's companions, to give us pleasure. Thank You, Lord." I pray.

Love is patient, love is kind [and] is not jealous; love does not brag [and] is not arrogant, does not act unbecomingly; it does not seek its own, is not provoked, does not take into account a wrong [suffered,]

1 Corinthians 13:4-5 NASB

**Lesson 31
We can all get along.**

Tonight, I watched Trouble and Daisy playing together. Daisy had a mouse toy and was meowing loudly over it. Trouble came up and rubbed noses with her, as if celebrating Daisy's joy over her mouse. Why can't people get along like that and not be jealous?

Snuggles and Rusty are also best friends. Sometimes they rough house together. Often Rusty will be asleep on the couch and Snuggles loves to lie down next to her. If two different animal species can be best friends, why can't people with different skin colors get along together?

We have a lot to learn from our pets.

There is neither Jew nor Greek, there is neither bond nor free, there is neither male nor female: for ye are all one in Christ Jesus.

Galatians 3:28 KJV

L'envoi

Cupcake died today. She had acute kidney failure and went downhill quickly. In the end, I had to have her euthanized rather than see her suffer. It is unthinkable to me to have any of my pets die alone, surrounded by strangers. I thank God for the sixteen years we had together. I held her in my arms and stroked her head as she passed quietly. I know that when my time comes, my Father in heaven will be holding me in His arms.

He will swallow up death in victory; and the Lord GOD will wipe away tears from off all faces; and the rebuke of his people shall he take away from off all the earth: for the LORD hath spoken it.

Isaiah 25:8 KJV

When I was a kid, I watched an old war movie. It was about a pilot who was to be shipped overseas. He had just met and fallen in love with a girl. Should they get married or not? He might not ever return. Should they perhaps bring a child into such a messed-up world? The girl's reply has stuck with me all my life: "I want all that life has to offer, all of its joy and all of its sorrow."

Never fear to love because it may end in pain. That would not be living.

L'chaim!

The End

www.ingramcontent.com/pod-product-compliance
Lightning Source LLC
Chambersburg PA
CBHW052150070526
44585CB00017B/2054